IN PURSUIT

A TRIBUTE...

MRS. MONJOYEE SHARMA PATGIRI

" In Pursuit" is a humble effort to encompass Life, Love, Nature, and Optimism, sharing the despair with all the ones who had lost their dear ones. With the past two years of uncertainty and sudden deaths due to Covid, there has been a prevalence of angst, fear, and stress, leading to maximum stroke-related deaths too. I feel that this pain should give us the strength to assert our capabilities, instead of lamenting and shedding tears and making our loved ones remembered fondly. Though everyone says to move on, it's never possible as this grief becomes an integral part of one's life.

This collection of poems "In Pursuit " is dedicated in the loving memory of my dear husband, Chandan Patgiri, on his First Death Anniversary.

I am grateful to the Founder of CWMA, Prof. Rachana Chakraborty and the team for giving me the opportunity to publish this book.

My heartfelt gratitude to all the versatile and talented personalities who have taken out their time to write a review of this collection.

Thank you

Monjoyee Sarma Patgiri

Contents

Contents

Prologue

Creative Writing Modern Age is always happy to support writers for a cause. We are happy to be associated with Mrs.Monjoyee Sarma Patgiri. She weaves life through her poems. Though the book is an ode in the memory of her better half we still get to know the different phases of her life. It is a beautiful memoir with wonderful illustrations all taken from the lenses of Late Mr.Chandan Patgiri.

From the founder's desk

Mrs. Rachana Chakraborty

Preface

In Pursuit

We are all in pursuit of something. At every stage of life, we play a different role. I have tried to reveal this nuance observed from my college days. In pursuit of joy, inner peace, knowledge, wealth, and divinity, one sets off to discover the unknown realms. The mystery of Death which changes the course of life of the loved ones finds expression here. I realize that this grief which becomes a part of our lives can be used in a positive and constructive way, cherishing those sweet moments. The soul connects and sends our good vibrations, the feeling comes that they are with us. My literary pursuits are my companion in solitude as I feel each word and relate with my husband's soul, keeping him alive in everyone's memory and thereby connecting with my readers whose motivation and appreciation add happiness.

Nature always alluded to me from my college days which were published in magazines and newspapers. and it finds its way in the poems, portraying the scenic beauties, and later I experienced mesmerizing moments in the lap of the Himalayas along with my husband, who had a passion for traveling and photography. Some of the photos that he had clicked are incorporated with the poems henceforth. My earlier love poems were inspired by the beauty of true love and still, I feel blessed that I have experienced it. True love surpasses physical constraints and attains spirituality. So, though the Death of a dear one shatters us yet it gives us more endurance to emerge stronger with the firm belief that the soul is our guiding spirit now. Even after his death, my love has surpassed the physical constraints, attaining spirituality.

Monjoyee Sarma Patgiri

(Poet)

Foreword

A sunrise beckons me to unravel its mystery

The soul is always in pursuit of joy, peace, contentment, and divinity as it embarks on a journey of life and beyond, leaving traces of memories behind. The poems in the book explore Nature's bounty, life, love, and death amidst hope and optimism.

Monjoyee Sarma Patgiri

(Poet)

Acknowledgements

Creative Writing Modern Age always believes that spoken words are always the best way of expressing your heart. We want to thank the author Mrs. Monjoyee Sarma Patgiri who had congregated all the beautiful memories with the help of spoken words. Her soul dedication to the lost soul is really serene. The book is a journey through those moments which they spent together.

We would also like to thank her late husband Late Mr. Chandan Patgiri whose photographs made the book more interesting.

Last but not least we would like to thank Notion Press for supporting the budding writers by helping them publish their books.

Mrs. Rachana Chakraborty

Founder & Mentor CWMA

1. THE CASCADE OF SOULFUL MYSTERY

The silvery sheets spread out, gushing down,
Spilling water beyond its barricade;
As the froth adorns like white laces
Over the mountainous banks of the cascade.
A wild glowing cinder through my soul ignites
Arousing the thought waves to connect;
Splashing the misty droplets of pristine love
Echoing the sweetest sound to reverberate.

The waltzing restless foaming whiteness,
Descends violently over the steadfast rocky way;
Unleashing the roaring storms of emotions
Till it meets the gentle waters of the bay.
Soon, the frantic heart dives into the calm river
Making the soul head and permeate with the sea;
Lost amidst cravings of ecstasy from a steady carousel;
Until the tidal waves ebb, to set the restless soul free.
If tomorrow comes, perhaps the soul emerge
From the depths of the restrained ocean floor;
Seeking to revert the wild journey of the cascade
Awaiting eagerly for the giant waves to hit the shore.

2. LIFE

Life with upheavals seeks a solution

So I approached ten-year-old Sam,
The youthful Ron and Uncle Tom.
Perhaps my curious mind calms.
Said Little Sam in a zestful way,
"Ah, Life! It's full of joy and fun
When I behold a rainbow in the sky,
With the birds soaring high,

The colourful flowers talk with me
The butterflies play hide and seek;
Life is a gift from God and Nature:
I shall preserve it with utmost care. "
Then added Ron in a merry voice,
"Life is a fountain of fresh water,
Quench your thirst when your heart desires
The ripples of passion keep bubbling,
But surely, foremost is our career-making. "
" Oh Life! It's a burden", sighed Uncle Tom.
" A burden too heavy---to carry.
Narrow is the passage of time,
I sway, I fall; a helping hand I seek
Age has made me a man too meek. "
Their varied views made me in silence ponder-
Life's meaning varies, it's only a murky meander.

3. CHARMS of NATURE

The wintry dawn lazily awakens
By the warmth of the glittering glow;
Snugly slithering through the foliage,
Bringing life to the fore.
Soon the tranquility is demolished
The environment is filled with a vocal blend;

With the twittering of the flamboyant birds
The crescendo of sweet music transcends.
In sportive zest, the fragrant breeze
Simpers as it passionately embraces me;
Enamoured am I, as in elation
The cascade of memories flees.
Indeed, scrambled years of joy and pain
Have endowed a glorious sanctity;
So let the soul's beauty be kept intact
To feel Nature's aura in this limitless greenery.

4. A LITTLE GIRL's WISH

Sometimes I wish to soar high—
High above to Thy abode,
Play with Thee and walk hand in hand,
And to control the world with Thy magic wand.
The wind at my command would blow,
Each life would be given a new glow,
Varied flowers at each stem would bloom,
And I would remove the very cause of gloom,

Reasoning power would be added more
Whence love would pervade each core.
Ah God! Hath I reigned over this World to pursue,
Joy, Peace and love – I would paint it with varied hues.
Alas! These wishes are limited to me
Only to fill my idle moments with glee.

5. BLISS FOR A YOUNG LASS

The moonlit sky, so calm, so bright,
Ah! It torments me all through the night.
No slumber entangles me
'cause everywhere thy reflections I see.
The simpering crescent and blinking stars
Erased even the smallest bar.
The memories then emanate through the mind
Exhorting me to rebind;
I wish the night would never end
And more with thee, I could transcend:
Through steps of joy we could reach
That place of eternal bliss.
But hark! The cock crows again
Which binds me in adamantine chains.
Then, beneath the warm jealous Sun
Those dreams pile up again to burn.

6. AWAITING THE DAY

That wintry evening, serenity pervaded
The fading sun retreating to it's occult shade
The busy birds flying back to their abode
All, an usual terrestrial mode.
Then, I was beside you, an onlooker
Of the approaching twilight.
But your eyes on me innovated queries-

Wordless queries not for the sensual ear.
My dormant heart did then answer,
Laying my head on your shoulder,
" My love shall be same through years
Though it might be perplexed by fears. "
Slowly aware was I, of the approaching night
As light failed to illuminate any sight.
Amidst this darkness, I heard you say,
" The day only steps,
When night paves the way. "

7. A MYSTERY

In moments of solitary contemplation
I often ponder;
Thy exquisite nature
Fills me with wonder.
Dost thou know! thou art precious,
Precious than any jewel,
In my world I keep thee hidden
As in my heart thou dwell.

No eyes can see, nor ears can hear,
Thy smiling face and sweet murmur.
No heart can feel that love within
Neither that depth enclosed in a rhythm.
In thine thoughts when I dwell
With joy, my mind doth swell.
Indeed, life has found a destiny
What though; if thou art a mystery!

8. MY SUNSHINE

The sunshine that day was precious
As I held you in my trembling hands,
Your soft touch made me feel complete
As papa smiled, " Our love child indeed. "
Through years as you grew, I remember
The sunshine we spent in the scenic bower,
You loitered in the garden in pursuit of-
Feeble grasshoppers and hued butterflies.
You tried to attach the plucked flowers again,
While papa's lenses captured your face in vain.
Still that tears' soaked sunshine, I remember
As your first teacher took you apart from me;
Your tiny hand reaching out for me gestured;
It's a single step to surge into a new vista, I figured.
Soon you learnt the nuances of human nature,
Imbibing ethics, setting goals, idolizing icons and peers.
What a pride to watch you grow!
As you try to fit into papa's shoes,
Rubbing my tears with words of concern,
Offering your strong hand to help me climb stairs-
I'm assured that I can surely make it through,
I may stagger but happy that by my side, I have you.

9. FROM THE SHIP's DECK

As the waves rise with the wind

My emotions soar to encompass;

The ever-changing possibilities

Of life's pursuit which for everyone differs.

From the cradle to the grave, the journey!

Sailing with an anchor to reach the harbor:

Weaving laces of tender threads across this anchor
Lest it drowns in the depths!
Like this river, always finding its own course,
Our love crossed many obstacles, to swiftly flow.
One day this river will meet the sea,
The horizon will widen just like our love will always be,
With years, when two souls merge silently
Invisible to many eyes, like losing the shore's sight
of the ocean, which is the ultimate soul's pursuit.
So my Love! Be prepared to view no shores, but a void;
As we keep sailing calmly above the depth of the ocean.

10. THE TRAVELLER

He sets his foot on the road again
Knowing that he needs to proceed on;
Living his life like a carefree vagabond
Only in love amidst trails unknown.
Like a tree, he never was meant to be grounded
But like a bird, he soared to heights with life's song,
Restless like the sea, lashing its waves, on the shore
Bringing back terrestrial residue of places he belongs.

Slowly, the traveller tired of his exploits now glimpses
The cliffs change their white caps on their crest;
The sun finally creeps down amidst the orange waves
A time of retreat as it cuddles for the midnight's rest.

11. THE PINE TREES

Let's walk you and I
Beneath the pine trees,
Feeling the alluring, whistling breeze.
My desire it is, to wait-
Wait to see, hear and feel
The wind, the Conjuror rushing
Amidst these limitless trees.
But your presence reminds me:

'tis only a lone journey to feel and view,
And not a mere pleasure for two.
I would go ahead, but you-
Alas! I decide to retreat,
Only to come back again, someday alone.

12. SHATTERED DREAMS

Like a volcano, my dreams erupt

In moments of great distress;
My defeated dreams are melted
And thrown out as lava.
When cooled, I try to gather
Bits of my dissipated dreams.
Perchance I can mould it
With joyous moments sometimes.
Alas! Broken pieces are forced to join
But will always carry a false splendour.

13. A MEMORY

Memories like froth of the waves
Lash my mind with great vigour;
I tend to sink in the soft sand with closed eyes.
That strange look of serenity, the aura of sadness,
A compulsion to leap into those arms-
The moment before separation, still haunts
A love, which will be a wonderful memory.

14. AN UNHEALED WOUND

You die once when your breath stops,
Leaving your loved one to die a thousand times;
'cause the peace of mind is forever lost.
The unheard puppeteers emerge to control the sways;
As your loved one entangles the strings and endow a sly escape.
Yet a life of pain, denial, angst and bitter loss
Drowns the loved one in a nightmare of dead reality.
Tears trickle viewing the bleeding frame, mocking the present.
The wound will last as long, love manifest itself
In silent sweet whispers of the heart; and the mind
Trying to restore its sanity, moves in pursuit of peace,
Lifting the wounded heart from the abyss of grief
Living with the scar, paying the price of love forever.

15. NIGHT MUSINGS

Lo! What are you staring at, my Love!
Waiting for my glimpse amidst the dark clouds!
The lightning has ripped the canopy into halves,
Flashing the glimpse of your anguished visage.
The thunder scares, as you clutch the balcony's pillar;
I know, you feel me hugging, as you sweetly simper.
The sound of rain on the rooftop creates magic,
As you envisage me galloping on horseback,
The sound of hooves mingle with the clatter;
Slowly the aura of silence engulfs the darkness

As the storm stops with diminished rage.
Now, you are desperate to view the starry sky,
When we'll talk through the endless night.
I still promise you a better sunshine tomorrow
Where you'll find me, but in your shadow
Our love will only grow in a different way
Surpassing physical entity embracing a new day.

16. TO CUPID

The soothing night as Zephyr endowed,
Made us steal glances, soft whispers flowed.
Cupid, thou hadst feared to compete!
Knowing that mortals will not praise thee;
Conspiring with ruthless Death thou snatched me.
So many things were left unspoken, as I saw her cry.
Lying on my cold breast, trying my breath to revive.
I watched her helplessly as they rubbed her Vermilion.
While I embarked on the last journey, my last rites done.
They took her to bathe and she wore the white robes

Which I couldn't bear. I detest to think of our plights:
As my ashes in an urn will only return, I loathe in vain.
But Cupid, hark! The sound of silence beckons
And she knows, it's me. She rises to spend the night.
Tonight the stars twinkle more brightly after the rains
I send her signs from amidst the moonlit sky
Promising her to be there in her dreams
Where we'll smile, cry, argue and complain.
Indeed, nothing beautiful comes without pain.
So music will give her solace as we'll listen to Bon Jovi,
"I want to lay you down on a bed of roses,
For tonight I'll sleep in a bed of nails. "
Hark Cupid! Thou art filled with envy again.

17. NO GOODBYE

The eerie silence of the mountains always allure
As in this abode, I seek your hand in despair,
I'm now at the mercy of the mocking clouds
Which always threw tantrums as you drove
Conquering heights amidst the snowy cliffs;
Just like you conquered my heart and ripped

The least fear of existence, so I won't let you
Bid 'Goodbye': until you rub the last tear
When I walk in solitude amidst these clouds
Feeling your presence, with the familiar odour.
Until you promise to wake me in the chilling morn,
From the bed of snowflakes which you have laid.
Until you again misplace the things I arrange,
Retorting at least with gestures at the words said.

18. AN ODE TO THE LOTUS

Amidst water bodies as you bloom in hues of purity
You often proclaim your tale to humanity.
As from the treacherous bog, you emerge strong
Inspiring humans to cling to the roots and be firm.
The muddy bog only creates resilience to evolve
More beautiful and pure, only to be divinely offered
To appease the deities so that wishes are bestowed.

Recollections of yore, and you brought utter bliss
To the Lotus-Eaters whom even Odysseus did seek.
Standing tall with grandeur despite the unsteady ripples
An epitome of pure beauty which, with divinity mingles.

19. ON A SPRING MORN

Come sunshine, let the bud bloom;
Come rain, let it get the succor and quench
The long thirst to blossom into a flower.
The beauty captivates all satiating eyes
When April showers wilt the soft petals
Unable to bear the brunt of its ferocity.
And lo! The next morning, serenity haunts
The fresh greens ready to soak the sunrays
Reflecting in the puddles; as grasshoppers
Compete with the hued butterflies in search
Of the flower, which could withstand upright
The night's storm and emerge as their saviour.

20. THE GATE

I walk a step behind you, lest you fall
Not like bygone days when you followed me.
I opened the gate to show you the arena
Where there were no laments but two loving hearts,

Mingling to merge into one soul and now-
I'm with you anytime, though none understands.
I enjoy it when I see you instantly turning around
With the hope of catching my glimpse in any stranger;
I try to rub that precious teardrop as you feel
The feather caressing your swollen face,
Each dawn I come into your dream to wake you
I know your day will be better then:
As you remember the glorious moments
I empower and add strength to you.
Death has relieved me of any earthly pain
And I'll wait for you until we meet again.

21. THE PERIL

The Falcon waits for its prey,
But she's grasping to take her last breath
Seeking divine intervention, with folded hands.
Her indomitable spirit is tarnished,
Before the ruthless predator;
Her frail body resists moving on,
Bogged amidst the marshy quagmire
With fading strength, realization dawns-
Why did she try to quench her thirst from a mirage?
A mirage that shone only in the sunlight!
Oh! She fails to move, she staggers in the dunes
With a last look at the perilous menace,
She resigned, though twilight blurred it's impeccable sight.

22. THE MYSTIC MOMENT

The majestic range unfolds the summit,
Just a tinge of pink before the first sunrays
Kisses the peak, changing its hue to whiteness.
The snow-capped mountain now emerges in purity
As two souls from different realms merge
To give a colourless hue and feel the divinity.

What though! The coldness freezes the bodies
True love will stand tall like the mountain
Which feels more like the sun's warmth,
Like the snow caressing, its frozen peak
To restore the fragments of sweet moments
Hidden forever in these mystic mountains.

23. THE DAY'S EARNER

With the setting sun adding an orange hue,
I was the lone spectator of this picturesque view.
Staggering with a burdened shoulder in the twilight

All that he could gather through, a despicable plight.
The huts of many were washed away by the waters
As lives were devastated by lightning and thunder.
This beautiful click also unravels an untold story
The day's earner struggling through a day of adversity.
Moving beyond barriers in pursuit of morsel and money
Realizing, that we get what we work for and that's destiny.

24. FINAL DESTINATION

Walking on a foggy lonely road
Unaware of the destination
The barking hounds scare me
Their menacing look eager to devour
A timid victim, but my steady steps
Perhaps forbade them to follow me.
Slowly the misty veil uplifts
And I could see the clear path
The cool pristine breeze surrounds,
As though those arms embraces me.
And with a renewed vigour, I look around
It's for me to find my own destination.
You had found yours and I blindly chose
to walk on your path, so I was lost.
But now I realize, this lonely path is mine;
The red blossoms of the Gulmohar shower, adding colours to the dull road ,
the dew-laden leaves gives succour ,
as the butterflies and little birds rejoice..

No longer am I, a lone stranger on this path,
Happy that no one can walk with me.
The glimpse of the high distant hills
As it touches the ever-receding horizon
Is where you stopped being captivated--
And now I shall walk happily to reach,
this mysterious destination and show you
The strength, the courage, the capability,
the direction your love has endowed on me.

The Traveller Speaks Through His Lenses....

Late Mr. Chandan Patgiri

"To leave in the hearts of people is not to die. "

This famous quote from Thomas Campbell has really found a true meaning, as he has left a mark in everyone's heart. His pursuit of adventure, the beauty of Nature, and the mysticism of the Himalayas have made him venture often into this realm, trying to capture it through his lens.

Asia's largest Flower Market

Incredible India

Incredible India

Incredible India

Incredible India

Chandan Patgiri
3 idiots awaited — at Incredible India.

01 04 2012

Majuli

At Pokhra, Nepal

The curves make the mountains more attractive

Gangotri

Serenity Speaks...Paro in Bhutan

Where the Streets beckon.. Thimphu in Bhutan

The mystic view after a successful trek

Sweet are the moments amidst Nature's tranquility

A ray of hope

A rainy day

The soul in search of divinity

Reviews From The Desk Of Authors And Poets

I

Nature is a manifestation of divinity. It exhibits kaleidoscopic hues every single moment, to make us aware of its divine power. But not all of us are fortunate to be a witness to all the glory of Nature. The author has endeavored to gift us some of those splendid hues of Nature, as seen and felt by her. Some of those ecstatic hues have been frozen in time, by her husband's photography and are a sheer visual delight. Her words bring her visions before us, in all their colours, to share her deepest feelings.

Dr. Dipendra Kumar Mazumder,
Faculty, National Academy of Broadcasting & Multimedia,
Delhi

II

I read beauty, my eyes, I feel beautiful, my heart, I live beauty, my soul

Each poem took me on a journey of passion, hope, sadness, and joy.

I can feel the life in each word that surrounds their souls.

The sunrises and the sunsets that open and close each day

Allowing this couple to share heart smiles.

There were times I had to stop reading to catch my breath.

My breath is back, and now, the journey begins once again.

Each time I read these words; it creates another beautiful feeling inside me.

By Grant Wass (poet)

I love to write poetry because it makes me feel. What I can't voice I choose to write. I lean on the dark end of the spectrum of life and death. My poetry helps keep me grounded with such thoughts. But, I am a soul...alive. My blood, my ink, my pen. So, my life is red in words.

III

"In Pursuit" is the greatest compilation of an emotionally rich composer Mrs. Monjoyee Sharma
Patgiri, which barely could keep your hearts away from weeping. It's

my great pleasure and an
honor to review this beautiful writing. This enormous collection is not just a set of alluring poems
but literally a guide for the younger generation on the topic of "Love". It's a lot to take home. I was
on a voyage to find the best composition I started to read but in vain. I loved each one of
them. At the start it was "Life" I thought the best, here comes " A Little Girl's Wish". No doubt
"My Sunshine" is the best I thought for a second. How can I settle for one? I love them all.
Reading this book made me want to become a soulful writer and a passionate lover like Mrs.
Sharma. The photographs by Mr. Patgiri have taken me to a whole new world, which blends so
well with Mrs. Sharma's writings which depict their souls in real life. Enjoyed every bit of it. Hope
that everyone who enjoys poetry will come across this masterpiece. Wishing her a successful
writing career to heal the souls with her talented positive vibe. Good luck!!

By Sachini Suryabandara

IV

EVERYONE CAN...

Filling the world with the green land of poems portrayed Is like granting open authority to all writers

What is real about us all, is the determination depicted. Ceasing author's rights of expression crops fighters. The opportunity everyone has is to utilize all chances. Having Strong dreams as composers is much better. Try out restless from the beginning to the tip just a base. When opposers think of confronting you. Sorry! but later, Enumerating ink in a pen pusher's weapon, is called the writer's triumph. We shall penetrate what is not expectable. Raise your emotions and feelings to relevance though rough. Raise your voice as much as you can, write about facts and truth Become an admiration and inspire such a simple plan. Admiring big to achieve is great of a narrow path Creative Writing Modern Age is my living testimony Everyone has got a talent.

By Ssekyanzi A Destiny.

UGANDA

V.

Monjoyee Sharma Patgiri is a great storyteller that creates incredible visuals that paint a picture in your mind. Moreover, they provide a relaxing, insightful power.

This writer takes you on a journey full of emotion. In pursuit is recommended for anyone who wants to escape to another world.

Andrew Scott – International Poet

VI.

Ms. Monjoyee Sharma Patgiri's " In Pursuit" is an endeavor at an engaged living, despite being signed by the tragedy of having lost her husband at a young age.

Many of her poems are set within the variegated beauty and motion of nature. In the midst of this she discovers or *finds* her loved one in joyous fortitude and meditative acceptance:

"True love will stand tall like the mountain

Which feels more like the sun's warmth

Like the snow caressing, it's frozen peak

To restore the fragments of sweet moments
Hidden forever in these mystic mountains."

(" The Mystic Moment ")

And:

" ... now I shall walk happily to reach,
this mysterious destination and show you
The strength, the courage, the capability,
the direction your love has endowed on me."

(" Final Destination")

These are but stray examples that affirm the vitality and compassionate sensibility of the poet.

The feelings in the poems are achieved with child-like simplicity. And it is this unadulterated honesty that will touch the chords of the readers

I wish Ms. Monjoyee Sharma Patgiri the very best on her onward journey as she forges the diversity of feelings and encapsulates them in the rhythm of words

Ranjit Kr Chowdhury.
Retired Professor and Head.
Department of English.
Cotton College (now Cotton University)

9 798887 496351

Printed by Libri Plureos GmbH in Hamburg,
Germany